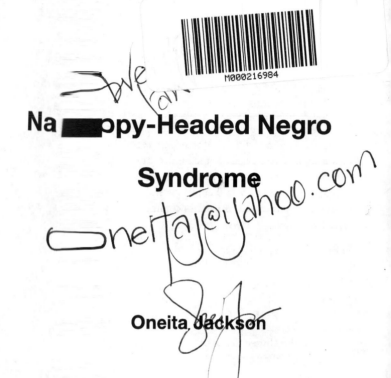

# Na███ppy-Headed Negro Syndrome

**Oneita Jackson**

*onerta@yahoo.com*

ANTI
GRAVITY

For permission requests, please address:
Antigrativy
7300 West Joy Road
Dexter, MI 48130

Published 2019 by Antigravity.
Printed in the United States of
America by Thomson-Shore.

Cover designs by Brian McNamara.
Book design by Thomson-Shore.
Hair by Jamie Farmer.
Emmanuelle Perryman, photographer
Alex Cruden, editor
Rhonda Nolen, Smart Tyme Consultants, manager
Watch, Swatch
Sneakers, Converse

21 20 19      1 2 3 4

ISBN: 978-1-943290-50-5
Library of Congress Control Number: 2018964382

## Also by Oneita Jackson

*Letters from Mrs. Grundy*

## Acclaim for *Letters from Mrs. Grundy*

"This is trademark Oneita Jackson, wherein she destroys all worldly pretense with wit and never wastes a word."

**DAVE EGGERS**, international bestseller

"If you want to know what *not* to do when giving service to customers, read this book!"

**ARI WEINZWEIG**, Zingerman's owner

"Oneita Jackson reminds us that grace, civility, and poise are still of import in the 21st Century."

**JAMES DEVORE CARTER II**, grandson of Ophelia DeVore, who founded the Grace del Marco modeling agency and a charm school in New York City during the 1940s

"A new Mrs. Grundy has been erected in the 21st Century by Oneita Jackson, and she comes from her troubled sleep to put some stick about. . . . If you get a whack, just assume that you deserved it."

**JON WOODSON**, author of *Summer Games* and *Endowed*, a *comic novel*

## Acclaim for *Nappy-Headed Negro Syndrome*, Preview Edition

"Damned funny, scalpel-sharp, and moves like a rocket."

**DAVE EGGERS**, international bestseller

"Her stories, hard hitting, and yet sensitive, and real—are worth the read."

**DENNIS W. ARCHER**, former mayor of Detroit

"*Nappy-Headed Negro Syndrome* creates, then perfectly fills, a niche in the national conversation taking place on race relations."

**RON BERNAS**, Shelf Improvement

"These are poetry of a high order. With an extraordinarily consistent tone, they are simultaneously transcendent and earthy. Every-day profoundly provocative. I think everyone should read them. (And it's wonderful to see pieces that give the reader credit for thinking.)"

**ALEX CRUDEN**, editor

"If you don't understand the racial climate going on in this country right now or are confused by it—if you have any questions, you need to read *Nappy-Headed Negro Syndrome*."

**RHONDA NORMAN**, MSW, Dayton, Ohio

*Nappy-Headed Negro Syndrome*

is dedicated to

**"the people at formal events who assumed we
were The Help."**

First Lady Michelle Obama

Tuskegee University, 2015

*Nappy-Headed Negro Syndrome*

is a handbook

to social etiquette

in the racially charged 21st Century.

It is a nonfiction work of

proceduralist recursive satire.

How to read:  In order.

I have lived in five U.S. cities, worked at 30-something jobs, hung out with people from all over the world. There are people who have always encouraged me and my ink pen, people interested in what I have to say. There are people who believe in my writing and love, appreciate, accept, and support me unconditionally.

I would run out of ink naming you all.

**THANK YOU.**

Jack Kerouac called it the "naked lunch, a frozen moment when everyone sees what is on the end of every fork." These moments of revelation are afforded by the greatest works of literature—Zen teaching stories, Sufi tales about Nasruddin, Aesop's Fables. Everyday life is delusional because human beings are heavily defended from reality: When there is a murder next door, they say, "This never happens in our neighborhood," and then there is the notion "I can do no wrong" that results in the delirious cases of road rage that are so puzzling and pervasive.

In Oneita Jackson's *Nappy-Headed Negro Syndrome*, we come face-to-face with the deepest taboos in the American psyche. Jackson, with humor and compassion, shows us the quality of the paradoxes that make us who we are— that make us so stubborn, dangerous, and unrepentant.

**JON WOODSON**, author of *Summer Games* and *Endowed, a comic novel*

My fare and I were having a conversation about education on the way to Detroit Metro airport. When he told me he received his Ph.D. from an Ivy League school, I laughed. He sounded right pompous sitting in the back of my taxicab. Though he was specific when he told me where he received his undergraduate and master's degrees—he got them from the University of Chicago and Northwestern—he spoke generally about where he received his Ph.D. An Ivy League school. There are eight Ivy League schools. "Harvard, Yale, Princeton, Dartmouth, University of Pennsylvania, Cornell, Columbia, Brown." I named them all and asked him which one. Harvard. "Then why didn't you just say you went to Harvard?" I said. "Because people make assumptions about me when I say I went to Harvard," he said. "You know you sound like someone who went to Harvard when you say, 'I went to an Ivy League school,' right?" He laughed. I told him he shouldn't try to manage people's reactions because they have a problem with the fact that he went to Harvard. It was just a fact.

We talked about assumptions and truth. I told him I was writing a book called *Nappy-Headed Negro Syndrome*, about identity, judgment, and assumptions—unconscious bias-type stuff. He could write one called *Harvard Syndrome*, I told him, because everyone has a syndrome: when someone comes to a conclusion about you and they don't know anything about you; constant communication of the idea that you are not precisely where you *are* supposed to be; when someone tells you you are outside of the context to which they think you belong.

I call mine Nappy-Headed for a few reasons. I don't look like my mother or her side of the family. They all have what regular black people call "good hair," even though there is no such thing as good hair or bad hair. My mother has boing-boing curly hair, and when I was a child, it was all down her back. I used to pull her curls and say, "Boing, boing" with each tug and release. My chemically untreated hair is not good or bad, it's nappy. Just a fact.

My use of the word "negro" recalls writers I studied as an English major at Howard University: Alain Locke (*The New Negro*), Carter G. Woodson (*Miseducation of the Negro*), W.E.B. Du Bois ("The Name 'Negro'"), Langston Hughes ("The Negro Artist and the Racial Mountain"), Richard Wright ("Blueprint for Negro Literature"). As a native of Dayton, Ohio, and graduate of Paul Laurence Dunbar High School, I honor the great American Negro poet, a Gem City native also, with every keystroke. I wink and nod at Dunbar. We both lived in Ohio, New York City, and Washington, D.C. He, too, was a newspaper editor, and he was friends with Orville and Wilbur Wright.

**Part One – Preview Edition  1**

**Part Two – Feedback  43**

**Part Three – Letters  59**

**Part Four – Quotes  97**

**Part Five – Stories  125**

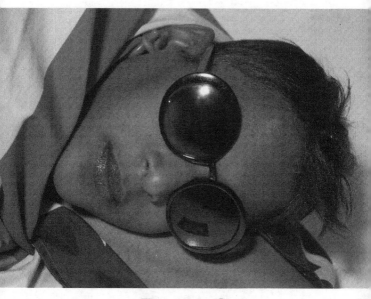

*Part One*

I am tired of people interrupting my existence
to inform me that I am black—whatever inferior
version of humanity they perceive that to be.

## Learning a Wing or Two

They don't take the EBT card at Neiman Marcus or
Saks Fifth Avenue.

They don't take it at the Detroit Athletic Club or
the Detroit Yacht Club.

They don't take the EBT card at Coach Insignia or
The Whitney, and they damned sure don't take it
at the Captain Jay's on Seven Mile and Gratiot in
Detroit.

This I learned from a manager in the Captain Jay's
parking lot.

My friend Paulette and I were hanging out; I left
the driving to her. We'd just come from the Pop-
eye's across the street—red beans and rice, two
drumsticks. I'm not often in the vicinity of a Captain Jay's, known in the streets for its crack chicken,
so when I see one, I start fiending.

Captain Jay's is not like mouth-wateringly good
like Sweetwater or City Wings in Detroit, or Fish
& Wings in Bessemer, Alabama, or Lou's Broaster
Hut in Dayton, Ohio.

It is kitschy good and I needed some Captain Jay's—
two chicken wings.

That is what prompted our impromptu information session on the chicken-wing payment policy: I
asked the woman how much was one wing.

Chris Rock.
Isaac Hayes.
I'ma gitchoo.

"What method of payment are you using?" she
asked, kindly.

She was standing a few feet from the car. I had
called out to her because the Captain Jay's digital
billboard did not list the price of an individual wing.

"What method of payment am I using?" I mouthed
to myself. This was an odd question, considering
we were not in a department store.

"Yes, because we don't take the EBT card."

They don't take the EBT card I don't have at the
chicken-wing joint. (Poor woman, she was trying
to save me from embarrassment.)

"They take it at the other Captain Jay's, but we don't take it here."

I smiled brightly—too brightly—nodded, and whispered.

"We have cash."

"You have an EBT?" she asked, misreading my glee.

"We have cash," I said a little louder, but not loudly enough.

I wanted her to come closer.

She did.

"We have money."

"Oh, OK."

"Now, how much is a chicken wing?"

She told me the price of the wings—three for $2.69, plus one dollar for frying—and offered, sweetly, "I'll take your order."

I placed my order for three wings and we proceeded to the drive-thru, where I paid with 14 quarters, one dime, one nickel, four pennies.

## The Motherfucker with the Shoes

The question was merely of onomastics, yet the Prescient One deigned to answer, communicating to me in so so certain terms that I was not now in a position to ask about, nor had I been invited to make observations of, such esoteric matter.

It was his shoes.

Very nice shoes.

What kind were they?

100% Certified Callipygian. Stamp here.

"Very expensive."

Very expensive shoes
Shoes so expensive,
have no name.

Name drop.

Gucci, Ferragamo, Yves St. Laurent
Shoes so expensive
my mirrored closet.

"Oh, then you can afford these."

We. Have. Arrived.

Detroit cab driver with Washington, D.C., big shot.

Shoe name get.
I forgot.
Airport, please.

## Job Search for Tomorrow

I haven't had to look for a job in 14 years, so I'm a little rusty on the process this millennium, but apparently it goes something like this: show up to a business unannounced, wear your sweatpants, take your six-foot-four German friend Yannick with you, ask for the person who does the hiring, and say you're on a first-name basis with her.

I was hipped to this new process when I went to Neiman Marcus looking for my friend Muffy.

My friend Muffy is the visual director at Neiman Marcus, Somerset, and she looks like a Muffy. When you say her name you have to say it like Thurston Howell III: "Muf-faaay." Muffy works all over the store and when I'm in there, I stop to say hello.

On this day I didn't see her, so I asked an associate to call her.

"Is Muffy here?"

"I'm not sure."

As the woman dialed, another Neiman Marcus associate waved to me from the escalator.

"That's my friend's mom," I whispered to Yannick.

"Who, René?" the associate asked, cradling the phone.

"Yes."

"Are you applying for a job?"

"No, Muffy is my friend."

"Who, René?"

René is a black woman, a sophisticated black woman. An elegant woman.

Muffy's not there.

"Would you like to leave a message?"

"No, Muffy is my friend. I live across the street from her."

"Oh, she's your *friend*?"

The Syndrome.

## Carded

Many years ago, the Neiman Marcus on Wisconsin Avenue in Washington, D.C., found a Howard University student buying a small item, a hat. The store didn't take my credit card and I didn't have enough cash. When I asked the associate what other methods of payment the store accepted, she asked if I had a Neiman Marcus card. I didn't. "That's it?" I asked. "Well," she offered reluctantly, "we take the Bergdorf Goodman card."

There is only one Bergdorf Goodman in the world. It is a New York City institution for insanely rich people who can afford insanely high prices for insanely nice clothes.

I didn't know Bergdorf Goodman's connection to Neiman Marcus, but I handed her my Bergdorf card, which they don't take at the Captain Jay's on Seven Mile and Gratiot in Detroit.

## Driving Miss Oneita

The doorman doesn't move.

The valet doesn't move.

I doesn't move.

They is impotent.

I is important.

I is in my yellow cab waiting for some service at the Detroit Athletic Club.

"What are you doing?" the doorman mouths from his place.

I is deaf.

I is dumb.

I is defiant.

And I is in the valet line.

"What are you doing?" he asks again when I doesn't move from my place.

"I'm having lunch is what I'm doing."

And I is waiting for him to open my door so I can make my entrance.

Doorman moves.

Valet moves.

I move.

"Thank you."

High-heeled black boots; fleur-de-lis tights; black dress; grandmother's vintage coat, Fordham Road, the Bronx; black shades.

I is fly.

My friend is a Grosse Pointe woman who belongs to the DAC; she and I are in a group that meets there. She was the first woman to integrate the group and had to fight to get in.

I didn't.

The man who runs it invited me.

(My friend loves when I tell this story.)

## Audio Visual

They don't get out much in Southfield, or much doesn't get out to them, it seems, because when I arrive at the movie theater, I am greeted by a Nappy-Headed Ticket Agent who takes one look at my Nappy-Headed ass and decides she will be starring in the role of Unsolicited Movie Reviewer.

Engagement with me beyond "enjoy the show," however, is simply unnecessary.

Roll tape.

Roll sound.

"Two tickets to 'Queen,' please," I say and turn to my Nappy-Headed friend. (We had dropped off my Curly-Headed and Straight-Haired Indian friends at the door.)

"That's a Indian movie!"

The movie I want to see is not the movie I want to see.

I stare at Little Miss Nappy and repeat sternly:

"Two. Tickets. To. 'Queen.' Please."

(For Blaxploitation flicks, we have Bounce TV, King's Dream, free, at last, thank God, almighty.)

Next time, I will not miss my cue to state the obvious.

"'Bollywood Movie Reviewer' starring Oneita Jackson as Miss Too Much, Take Two":

Roll tape.

Roll sound.

"Two tickets to 'Queen,' please."

"That's a Indian movie!"

**"YOU'RE A TICKET AGENT!"**

## Guest Who?

Anna Wintour would have been pleased.

I certainly was. I looked like I stepped off the cover of Vogue magazine and was staring at myself a little too long.

This self-adulation was interrupted by a woman who had spilled something on her dress. She looked like she belonged on the cover of a Walmart circular and should have taken more care.

We were in the powder room at a little club in Grosse Pointe. It was so exclusive that the only people who looked like me were wearing black-and-white service attire and were parking cars, serving food, and clearing tables.

I helped the woman in distress get herself together and that is when things became interesting.

*Event*
Annual black-tie dinner for a private Detroit club.

*Access*
I am the date of a gentleman from Chicago.

*Me*

Dupioni silk gown, chocolate A-line, velvet tessellated overlay.

Silk halter, chocolate cowl neck with ruching at back zipper.

Stuart Weitzman cowboy boots, chocolate-leather front, black pony-hair back, chocolate-leather lacing at calf.

Long-sleeve mesh turtleneck.

Chocolate Bottega Venetta intreccio sunglass case, handbag.

Short, chic haircut.

*Her*

Rayon-polyamide tank top, black.

Nondescript ankle-length skirt, black.

Square, low-heel pumps, black.

Blunt blond bob.

*Transaction*

"We've been waiting for you."

*Furrowed brow. I don't know this woman. Wait, I'm Oneita Jackson. My reputation precedes me. But wait, I don't know this woman.*

"You've been waiting for **me**?"

*Wait, she must know my date. He's from Chicago and his reputation precedes him, but I don't know this white woman.*

"Yes, we've been waiting for you."

*You can't be waiting for me 'cause I 'on' even know you, lady.*

"You've been waiting for **ME**?" I say, pointing to myself.

"Yes, we've been waiting for the band to start."

"Is there a band?"

(Get clue here.)

"Are you with the band?

(Miss clue there.)

"No, I'm a guest."

Apparently, I was late.

And I don't even look like Thornetta Davis.

## Black People Knit

I said I was a knitter, but that's not what she heard.

We were at a loud party at my friend's house in West Village and I was the only One.

It didn't matter that we were having a polite and interesting conversation, one of those getting-to-know-you, how-do-you-know-so-and-so (read: Why are YOU here?) conversations, where my announcement would have been inappropriate, moreover, inappropriate, moreover, awkward, off-topic, out of context, strange.

Arresting.

"I'm a nigger."

What dumb-ass nigger says that at a white-people party?

No nigger says that at a white-people party.

No Head Nigger in Charge knitter. Hood-rat knitter. Church-folk knitter. Weed-smokin' knitter. Educated knitter. Politically correct knitter. Hip-hop knitter. White-people-loving knitter. Avant-garde knitter. President of the United Fucking States knitter.

No knitter says that.

I knew she thought I said that other word because she didn't react. Usually, when I announce myself as a "knitter," people say something.

"I'm a knitter, too."

"My grandmother knits."

"I learned to knit when I was a kid."

"My aunt knits my kids sweaters."

"We have a stitch-and-bitch."

"What do you knit?"

"Do you knit hats?"

"Can you knit me a scarf?"

"How long have you been knitting?"

"Where do you buy your yarn?"

"What are you working on?"

"How many projects you got goin'?"

"Do you knit on straight needles or circulars?

"There's a yarn shop around the corner."

"Do you knit the American way or Continental?"

"Have you ever knit a pair of socks?"

"Do you shop at the Wool & the Floss?"

"My mom taught me how to crochet."

"I heard knitting is coming back."

"My sister-in-law does needlepoint."

"My husband's cousin makes beautiful quilts."

"You're a knitter?"

They say something.

She said nothing.

It was her blank pale face that gave me pause. I was

a few sentences in before I came to. No questions forthcoming, I looked at her askance.

"Wait: Did you just think I said I was a nigger?"

"Yes."

Ladies and gentlemen, tonight's Golden Globe for **BEST PORTRAYAL OF A POLITICALLY CORRECT WHITE WOMAN IN AN UNCOMFORTABLE SITUATION** goes to the horrified little suburbanite at a house party in Detroit.

I placed my hand on her shoulder, amazed by her composure.

"Girl, you are good! That was so polite."

"I said, 'knitter,'" I said, and started air-knitting.

We laughed and laughed and laughed.

It's not funny.

## Fecal Matter

*Case. Point.*

"Why do you black people always get so offended by shit?"
*Cute White Guy from Berkley, in front seat of taxi cab, headed home after St. Patrick's Day parade in down-town Detroit, 18 minutes into cab ride.*

"Because y'all always say stupid shit."
*Oneita Cab Driver, on I-75 north, just past the Clay/ Grand Blvd. exit.*

*Stupid. Shit.*

"How do you know about Amici's Pizza?"
*Cute White Guy from Berkley, in front seat, headed home after St. Patrick's Day parade in downtown Detroit, 2 minutes into cab ride. Picked up on the cor-ner of Michigan & Trumbull, he asks first to go to the Atheneum Hotel to get his belongings, then, "Can you drive me to Berkley?" Oneita Cab Driver responds: "You mean 'Berkley,' like Amici's Pizza?"*

*Getting to Know You*

"What do you do when you're not at work?"

*Oneita Cab Driver, 13 minutes into cab ride, after talking with the Cute White Guy about the parade, which draws hundreds of thousands of people.*

*Education*

"Have you ever heard of Brother Rice?"
*Cute White Guy from Berkley, in front seat of taxi cab, headed home after St. Patrick's Day parade in downtown Detroit. He tells Oneita Cab Driver he is a coach at the all-boys Catholic high school.*

"My son went to U of D Jesuit."
*Oneita Cab Driver, 14 minutes into cab ride.*

*Lowest Common Denomination*

"How did you pay for that?"
*Cute White Guy from Berkley, in front seat of taxi cab, headed home after St. Patrick's Day parade in downtown Detroit, 15 minutes into cab ride, upon learning Oneita Cab Driver's son attended an all-boys Catholic high school on the west side of Detroit.*

*High. School.*

"I wrote a check."
*Oneita Cab Driver, 16 minutes into cab ride.*

*Class*

"Tell me why you're asking me how I paid for my son's education."
*Oneita Cab Driver, 17 minutes into cab ride. She has had enough of this shit.*

## How Did You Pay for That?

robbed bank

danced nights

sold crack

sold loosies

sold stamps

sought sugar daddies

(worked hard)

(worked not)

sold dinners

stole hundreds

stole thousands

started church

impersonated pastor

drove cab

edited copy

wrote columns

called mom

begged uncle

worked nights

worked weekends

facilitated deals

snitched once

snitched twice

offered child

arranged meetings

sang jazz

wrote rhymes

spit verses

borrowed heavily

waited tables

blackmailed media

sponsored terrorism

severed ties

DIRECT DEPOSIT

solved problems

petitioned kim jong un

started nonprofit

swindled nonprofit

surveyed land

engineered deals

created partnerships

facilitated meetings

organized workshops

wooed gilbert

courted quicken

exploited opportunity

placed bets

sold heroin

cheated IRS

smuggled diamonds

rustled cattle

peddled m & m's

wrote books

ordered deaths

sought grants

asked friends

petitioned family

sacrificed everything

sacrificed nothing

sold weed

sold out

sold lies

sold dreams

printed cash

yen

pesos

renminbi

euros

amex

visa

master charge

diner's club

money orders

used EBT

who said I paid, anyway?

can a nigger get a scholarship?

# ADVISORY

Drunk white people scare me.

Drunk white people in downtown Detroit on
Opening Day and St. Patrick's Day scare me.

Drunk white people in the back
of my ride scare me.

But a drunk white woman in the back of
my cab calling me outta my name

at three o'clock in the morning

is not scary.

It's disrespectful.

You keep calling me "Baby Doll" while
I keep telling you "I'm Oneita."

I'm a little sensitive, Miss Daisy.

## Oneita Big Dummy

I got pulled over in Grosse Pointe.

Everyone in Detroit knows you do not speed through Grosse Pointe.

You can do 55 on Jefferson, but you better slow your roll when you cross Alter Road.

Grosse Pointers—from all five Pointes—do not speed in Grosse Pointe.

Grosse Pointe police officers do not speed in Grosse Pointe.

No one speeds in Grosse Pointe.

I was speeding in Grosse Pointe.

ROOOORP. ROOOORP.

LIGHTS! CAMERA! ACTION!

(And I'm singing, "I'm sorry, Miss Jackson.")

The officer is at my window.

My hands are stretched straight out, almost touching the steering wheel, my E.T. Phone Home fingers spread wide.

"Why are you holding your hands up?"

I am a dark-brown woman in a beyond-lily-white upper-class suburb of Detroit, where just a couple years ago, a few police officers forced black men to sing and dance and make strange noises, and this white man is asking me why I am dramatically demonstrating to him that I am not a threat.

It was a natural reflex and I do not understand the question.

## Reflections

When I look in my mirror

In the morning,

I see Oneita.

When I look in my rearview mirror

later, I see red, white, and blue lights

and I see a police officer.

Flashing.

Lights.

HANDS ON THE WHEEL.
DON'T MOVE AN INCH.

When the police officer

looks at me,

he sees a scofflaw:

40

in

a

25.

Flashing.
Lights.

DO NOT TOUCH THE WINDOW.
DO NOT GRAB YOUR PURSE.

OFFICER APPROACHING. SIT STILL.

"Why are you holding your hands up?"

the privilege of obliviousness

I'm real confused, I

always speak truth, I

don't want to die, I

today I lie, I

Uhhh ...

...

...

...

Ummm...

"There's nothing there, officer."

I am a Generation X black woman in Grosse Pointe.

He is an X+ white police officer.

With a gun.

This is the United States of America.

"Yes, sir."

"Yes, sir."

"Yes, sir."

25

in

a

25.

Oneita Big Happy:

He lets me go!

*Part Two*

Why does my truth offend you?

## Words, Power

"Why are you calling it that?"

*Very Important Negro Writer, about the title* Nappy-Headed Negro Syndrome. *She lectures Oneita about the pejorative use of the word "nappy" in the African-American community. "You should change that," she says.*

## Sticks, Stones

"You might want to think about changing that title."
*Very Important Writer. She tells Oneita the word*
*"nappy" evokes painful memories from her childhood.*

## Books, Covers

"So, how are you writing something titled Nappy-Headed ... clearly from a straightened head perspective?"
*Very Important Member of the Nappy Bourgeoisie, who hadn't cracked the book's spine.*

## Gotcha

"Captain Jay's is on Seven Mile and Gratiot."
*Young black man, whom Oneita knows to be a critical thinker, reacting to the Preview Edition, which says the chicken wing joint is on Six Mile and Gratiot. He is correct: It is not. It is the one error he sees in the book, he tells her.*

## Gotcha, Gotcha

"Captain Jay's is on Seven Mile and Gratiot."
*Older black woman, in a dentist's office, after reading
the Preview Edition. It is her only response to the book.*

## Literati

"Who reads your books?"
*African-American radio host, to Oneita, during an interview.*

"People who read books."
*Oneita.*

"How are book sales?"
*Polite people.*

"They'd be better if the people who asked about book sales actually bought books."
*Rude Oneita.*

"How are book sales?"
*Nice Detroit bookstore owner to Oneita, an African-American woman who lives in Detroit and writes non-fiction. The bookstore specializes in nonfiction books, books by African-American writers, books by Detroiters, and books by women. The African-American-owned bookstore does not carry Oneita's books.*

"Great!"
*Polite Oneita.*

## Privilege of Obliviousness

"I'm looking forward to reading more of your fiction."
*Publisher of a university press, rejecting Oneita's manuscript of the Preview Edition. Oneita tells the kind white woman that the stories depicted are real, no disclaimers. "This book is nonfiction," Oneita says. "That's what I meant," the white woman says, unconvincingly.*

## Class

"I thought you were being thin-skinned."
*Oneita's friend, a middle-age white man from Grosse Pointe, responding to an account in the Preview Edition where a doorman at the private Detroit Athletic Club was rude to Oneita when she tried to valet her cab. "A white cab driver would have been treated the same way," he says. Oneita never mentioned race in the piece and she does not bring it up during the conversation with her friend. "It just rubbed me the wrong way," he says.*

## Do You See What I See?

*"'The Queen'* with Helen Mirren is not an Indian movie."
*Oneita's middle-age, white male friend from Grosse Pointe, after reading the Preview Edition. In* Audio Visual, *Oneita and her Indian friends see a movie titled "Queen." It is a Bollywood movie with an Indian cast. Helen Mirren is not Indian and she is not in the movie.*

# The Jerk

"You show what it is like to grow up poor, but educated."

*West Coast magazine publisher, writing to Oneita, after
reading the Preview Edition. Oneita did not grow up
poor. She asks the middle-age white man how he reached
that conclusion. "Something I read," he says. "What?"
Oneita asks. He reads the book again and tells Oneita
he finds no evidence to support his conclusion that she,
like Steve Martin, was born a poor black child.*

## Why Black People Always Get So Offended By Shit

"Let me ask you something, O. Do you look for this stuff?"

*High school classmate, after reading the Preview Edition. He was the coolest white boy at Paul Laurence Dunbar, Oneita's mostly black high school in Dayton, Ohio, and challenges the normalcy of Oneita's Syndrome experiences.*

"You don't have to—all black people, all people of color have these experiences. No one goes around looking for white people to say something stupid to them when they are just minding their business. You think I am looking for a white woman to insult me when I'm at an event enjoying myself?"

*Oneita, going off on her high school friend.*

## Inconvenient Truth

"It was better than good. It did what I'm assuming you wanted it to do, it made me think.

Sure I laughed, but not the way you or your non-white friends would. Mine was an uncomfortable, oh damn laugh.

I can't laugh at this stuff the same way you can. I'm the one that's supposed to be able to help fix it. I'm the one that gets it, yet has still said and done racist crap.

The one who has racism creep into his thoughts. When I'm inconvenienced or cut off.

The way someone drives. The way they dress. The way they talk or walk or whatever it may be. It's disgusting that I allow it to live in a dark corner of my mind.

It's embarrassing to admit. I hate it.

Love is what I want. I fight for it in my life daily. I know it can win, but now and then the confederate cell in my mind tries to take a stand for ignorance.

I know that the more people that I meet and know and learn from, the more that cell is exiled.

More than you asked for.

More than I've ever admitted to anyone.

I hope that doesn't change our ability to build a friendship. Knowing that I have a sliver of hate deep in me.

I suppose you've lived enough to already know it's there.
Is it there in everyone? Do they all have this fight?"
*Mike Kosh, Facebook friend, after reading the Preview Edition. Oneita has waited two-and-a-half years for this type of response.*

*Part Three*

Where have all the racists gone?

When I was a Detroit Free Press opinion columnist, my readership was diverse.

Every kinda people read O Street, which was based on my observations about life as a nonnative Detroiter, a mother, a foreign car driver, bus rider, churchgoer. I threw parties for my readers, and if you unsuspectedly walked into the room you would have no idea why all those kinds of people—young, older, Detroiter, suburbanite, City of Detroit worker, corporate worker, public school parent, private school parent, Christian, Muslim, artist, scientist, small business owners, farmers, hoodrats, educators, single mothers, married couples, gay couples—were in the same room.

I used to receive interesting e-mails from people, especially when I wrote about national and international topics, and the rare occasions I wrote about the idea of "race." Letters often revealed people's hatred, ignorance, anger, and assumptions about, or lack of exposure to, cultures to which they did not belong. Many readers made assumptions about who I was and who I wasn't and about things I did not write.

One time I wrote a column about my son's 16th birthday week. I set up five dinners with friends so he could have conversations with them about their professions. "Mom, you have me going to all these meetings," he complained. I told him to look at the "meetings" as free food for a week. At the end of the week, I threw a party to celebrate my 16th anniversary of motherhood. It was the column that engendered the greatest response of my writing at the newspaper. My writing was often controversial because of its unapologetic truth, but this piece seemed universal in its appeal. One reader sent this, though: "Why not a discussion with his Father on the responsibilities of being a parent?" "He did talk with his father," I wrote, "who is in Washington, D.C."

I received e-mails from racists who were being their unapologetic racist selves, and I respected them for knowing who they were. I received e-mails from racists who did not know they were racists and those people scared the shit out of me.

I was often asked by well-meaning white people to clarify something about their idea of the universal black cultural experience.

"This stuff just tears (as in 'rips') me up," one man wrote. "The mom of the kids I tutor has a sister who has three kids by three different men, now all in prison. The sister and other family members give her a bad time because she and her husband are giving their kids an education and doing well, economically. Duh! That's bad? If doing that is a White thing, what's a Black thing? I don't get it. Is that what they want? It's not White and Black, it's smart and dumb. How can we change this?"

I responded to the reader that he and I had the same basic values and that I rejected the idea of being educated as a white thing, and I did not know any people like the family he described.

"You've made me feel a lot better, O," he wrote. "We get the impression that people like Colin Powell, Condie Rice, my neighbor across the street, and you are exceptions. That's the problem with those nasty stereotypes, but I had no idea there were groups of people with a 'profile' like yours who grow up together. That's wonderful! Bless you for all you do."

Bless his heart.

A well-meaning white woman asked me to clarify something the Rev. Dr. Joseph Lowery said at former President Barack Obama's inauguration in 2009. She was offended because she did not understand something, which she described as racist.

"Hi Oneita! Like the rest of the world, I was riveted by yesterday's historic events. My heart soared when I heard my staunch Republican, racist father claim he is 'okay with this, it's a day that makes me proud to be American.'

I've written you in the past and love your O Street column, though I'm not too blog savvy so I've never been there.

I need your help understanding something from yesterday's events. When the Rev. Joseph Lowery concluded his benediction with what I see today in the Freep is a well-known rhyme, the roomful of women I was with were all extremely put off. Offended. Consider, a moment, that none of us are 'black churchgoers,' so this was our first time to ever hear that rhyme. Perhaps there was some laughter from the crowd, but for the millions of us who were not in on the 'inside joke' it can only be considered blatantly racist. It seems so counter-Obama—using old stereotypes like that. Can you enlighten me so I feel less offended and more understanding of that jarring moment on an otherwise glorious day?"

Here is how Lowery concluded the benediction:

"We ask you to help us work for that day when black will not be asked to get in back, when brown can stick around, when yellow will be mellow, when the red man can get ahead, man; and when white will embrace what is right."

It is a reference to a Big Bill Broonzy song:

> *This little song that I'm singing about*
> *People you all know it's true*
>
> *If you black and gotta work for a living, now*
> *This is what they'll say to you,*
>
> *"If you's white, you's all right,*
> *If you's brown, stick around,*
>
> *But if you's black, oh, brother,*
>
> *Get back, get back, get back."*

Here is my response:

"Thank you for writing, ma'am.

The answer to this question could be about a month's worth of blog posts and years of conversations.

Right now, I don't have time to give your e-mail the consideration it needs, but I want to give you an answer anyway: finding out about the laughter, instead of being offended by what you didn't understand, is a good start.

One day I may do a series of blogs on just this kind of thing you are asking.

I thank you for thinking enough of me to ask this question, but short of a lecture or series of critical essays . . . You should just laugh.

Barack Obama did."

I sent the woman links to Big Bill Broonzy's song and told her I hoped it help her understand the historical context of what Lowery said. I also told her that it wasn't racist—merely mentioning skin color does not make something or someone racist—and that she shouldn't be offended.

A few days later, I received this from her:

"One of my dear friends from college, who I basically communicate with through Facebook now, tagged the Rev. Lowery prayer as her highlight of the day. This from a woman who campaigned and canvassed hard for President Obama (so there were many other highlights, I'm sure) . . . so I re-watched the clip, knowing it's context, and it is a funny and even tender moment.

Keep the conversation going . . . that's a good step!"

The following letters arrived in my inbox and mailbox from 2007-2010. I include the letters, presented exactly as they were written, because I hope to inspire us to have honest conversations about humanity, respect, and dignity and to consider the racial significance in communication. Donald J. Trump is the president of these great United States and he inspires much tumult and shouting about the ideals of American identity and American civility. These letters were written when George W. Bush and Barack Obama were the presidents. As you will see, my fellow Americans, we have a lot to talk about.

Dear Ms. Jackson:

I cannot believe what I read in your column about your beloved Toyota vehicle. Do you have your head in the sand on *O Street?*

Reason for my question are three things:

1. Have you never thought of, or heard of—"You scratch my back and I'll scratch yours?" Translation: you buy what I manufacture (American cars) and I'll buy what you produce?

2. Did you ever stop to think that if you went to Japan for a job what kind of employment you'd be looking at? The highest position - secretary. They do not have any respect over there for a smart woman.

3. You and I were too young to have lived through the bombing of Pearl Harbor by the Japanese on December 7, 1941. And you still buy their products?

I know you'll say that the Japanese have car manu-facturing plants here in the U.S., but do you know the bottom line? Where does the profit go? Not the United States or better yet, Michigan. No, it goes to Tokyo, Japan.

Perhaps you can have fun driving your wonderful Toyota to the unemployment office.

Wake up as all Americans should.

*Because of my home training, my standard was to respond to Detroit Free Press readers with civility, compassion, and grace. I do not work at a newspaper now. The responses in bold are things I would say if I had no home training.*

**Americans make big ugly cars. I do not like big ugly cars. I do not buy things I do not like. Japanese make cute cars, but I have never bought a Japanese car. I have never owned a Japanese car. Perhaps you can have fun driving your big ugly American car to the library to educate yourself about vehicle manufacturers on other continents. Start with Europe.**

Greetings Oneita,

Good for you driving a car that you've owned for 19 years. It's sensible & practical and shows you have a good grasp of a concept that many Americans have forgotten which is to buy what you can afford.

My guess is you are driving a 1979 Toyota Corolla. Am I close?

**No, my car is not Japanese, not compact. You *are* onto something about affordability, though: My mother bought my car; it lasted 317,000 miles.**

After reading your 'why I dive a foreign car' I was at first angry then pity took over when I saw your picture.

A few years ago an Asian car manufacturer stated that that the reason the quality of American cars is so poor was that American manufacturers had to hire so many Afro-Americas and women.

Yes this manufacturer apologized emphatically and the statement was forgotten. No Jesse Jackson, no Rev. Sharpton boycott; perhaps they received forgive me money, who knows.

This statement was wrong on all levels but the sentiment was a projection of how these manufacturers feel about blacks and women.

There was also pity that the education system has let you down or you fail to take advantage of the system. Seems that you can not use your cognitive abilities to analyze that buying foreign products hurts us a country but you as a member of a minority and gender group that is held in such disdain. The Asian's have a saying that you will never go poor by over estimating the stupidity of the American people. I pity that you represent that statement.

**Do the Germans say that, too?**

Hi Oneita ~

I've read a couple of your columns lately about teaching respect and tolerance to your son. I'm trying to deal with a recent incident with my son-in-law who is African American. I'm caucasion and thought the relationship, though not as warm and fuzzy as I would have like, was going well enough. Even though I spent time in their home taking care of my grandaughter for 2 weeks at a time (by request to help defray expense of babysitters), giving them a date night, he just didn't feel the need to be sociable with me. I've always done whatever I could to help out, which included fixing them a meal for when they come home from work, picking up the house (occasionally bigger cleaning jobs b/c they didn't seem to notice the gross condition of the stove & refrigerator) and I've always been smiling and friendly and low key in his home and non judgemental, but he never seemed to 'share the love'. My daughter & I had a huge falling out b/c one day out sheer frustration with their slovenliness (which they seemed to be passing on to my 2 yr old grandaughter) I vented in an email that I sent to both of them at work. My daughter immediately hired a nanny and after we had a heated phone conversation about the email, and she insisted that I apologize to her husband. She strongly defends his behavior and shows no remorse over her verbal attack on me. She didn't communicate directly with me for a week after I left town, only via text or email. She did come visit for a weekend for my 65th b'day a couple of weeks later, so that made me feel our relationship is repaired for the most part. But her husband, who I've apologized to via text along with a couple other messages to thank him for my daughter travelling out of state for my b'day, is still standoffish. They were in town this past weekend and he limited seeing us to less than a 1/2 hour. What do you think of the situation? I'd greatly appreciate any suggestions you can make. Sincerely,

p.s. I have never been a racist even though I grew up with parents who had very strong racist feelings, but I really think mixed race marriages are doing more harm than good. My grandaughter is absolutely beautiful but I think African American men are doing their race a dis-service by diluting it, this WILL eventually cause the race to become extinct, don't you think??

**You know what I think?? I think love is a beautiful thing. I also think that although you might not be a racist, even though you grew up with parents who had very strong racist feelings, you would win an Emmy for playing one on TV.**

Hey, this is cool that you're keeping in touch. Loved the Sunday column about just acknowledging people with a smile and/ or hello promotes positive vibes. I always felt that way when I worked at a company where the atmosphere was so unconnected.

Hope you don't mind hearing an update on the fam...I had to go to Indy to cover for the nanny who was on her honeymoon, so I tried your suggestion to ignore the fact that my son-in-law didn't attempt to be sociable with me. His b'day was the day before I arrived, so I brought him a Mary J cd with the duo of 'One' that she does with Bono. He politely thanked me for the cd and the card I sent. That was pretty much our interaction for the 4 days I was there. I babysat while they went to work and again when I suggested they go out for their anniversary; spent an afternoon helping my daughter weed their yard that was much needed (her father's comment to her). I'm disappointed that my son-in-law still has the 'wall' up, but I guess you're right, accept him as he is and get over it.

**I know you're not a racist, though you grew up with parents who had very strong racist feelings, but do you think that that wall your African-American son-in-law put up might**

just be a response to your ideas about nigres-
cence and the fact that you think mixed-race
marriages are doing more harm than good
and that you think African-American men
are doing their race a disservice by diluting it?

Really, Oneita, do you do any proofreading before publishing? You sound just as bigoted as the guy you were trying to push the NYT on. "That Other Paper" also is a newspaper. If he had offered it to you, what would your response have been?

**I would have politely declined because I read That Other Paper, too: The Detroit News had much better news coverage than the Detroit Free Press.**

Just a gentle nudge. When you refer to yourself as "Rep. of Black Folk", isn't that a tad racist? How about being the Rep. of U.S. Folk? I imagine and hope that, long after I'm gone ( I am seventy years of age), there will be a world of totally integrated "Folk". All blended together and oblivious to the color issue. At least, that's my inspiration for this tired old world. I will check in to your suggested blog and may lurk about, or not. I do enjoy your writing. Why else would I be contacting you?

**Would you have thought it a tad racist if I had said I was the Rep. of Short Folk or Rep. of Right-Handed Folk or Rep. of Happy Folk or Rep. of Female Folk? What if I had said I was the Rep. of Knitters? Obliviousness *is* the issue. The color of my skin is not.**

Dear Oneita, I really enjoyed your column this morning and got to thinking. Do I infuse race in my discussion of politics etc..? I realised that I did. I reflected on a number of times I said, "this black woman I know" or " a couple of black friends". Its almost imposible not to have that reflex being born in this country and especially this city. Growing up in a working class family I was exposed to a great deal of racial insensitivity, but I never thought my parents were full bore racists. It seems to me that human social evolution has been plagued by the intense identification with our tribe. Tribalism is a curse. A component of wars! How do you solve it? Well anyway, I thought being a sixty three year old retiree, I was the only one enamored by the Talking Heads and David Byrnes lyrics." Same as it ever was, same as it ever was."

**If your parents were not full bore racists, why do you think tribalism is a curse?**

I enjoyed 99% of your articles;I was a high-school counselor and the graduation ceremony you just described ( 6/15/08 article) happened during every ,single ceremony we held.also so loved the funeral of the 'homeless" man. The one article over the year that I didn't agree with (who cares?) was the one about you and the dear mechanic "friend." When he referred to you as "you people" MAYBE he meant drivers who want their cars fixed for almost no money and question the final repair figure. I have always felt mechanics charge too much and they could include me in the "you people" category. Please keep up the great articles.

**Why do you think MAYBE I wanted my car fixed for almost no money?**

"We don't read your column because of what you are. But the NRA cartoon caught our eye. I and my friends and neighbors recently bought pistols, not because we're afraid of them being taken away but because there's going to be a Negro species in the White House. With you Negro species being prone to crime and violence, with a Negro species as the president, you're going to try to get away with more crime and violence and also try to dominate this country. We'll be ready for you!!!!"

**Guess what? I'll be ready for you, too. I just bought two packs of pens, not because I am afraid of you, but because I am actually going to *use* them. And where are you from? Don't they teach manners on your planet?**

Have you ever written a sentence that didn't contain at least two first-person singular personal pronouns? While it's true that I don't often read your stuff, I don't recall seeing one.=

**Reading is fundamental.**

**I told the person that I had, indeed, written a sentence that didn't contain at least two first-person singular personal pronouns and sent a copy of this piece about the word "nigger," which received a Detroit Free Press Best Column/Commentary award and gained international attention: A radio host called the newsroom from Budapest, Hungary, to interview me about it.**

*The Undead N-word*

The pragmatists at the NAACP have attempted to execute something linguistics experts, anthropologists, sociologists and other "ists" will tell you is impossible: send a word to its final resting place.

Now that the worldwide spectacle is over—the Princess Diana-like funeral for a multilayered word that will always have a pulse—Oneita the Language Provocateur has questions.

How do you convince yourself that you can David Copperfield a word from a language just because you are discontented with civilization?

You can't.

Because language is a direct reflection of humanity. To embrace a full humanity, you must have a full language. Erasing a part of the language by magical thinking, even one wrapped up in as much pain, ignorance and controversy as the one purportedly buried, is tantamount to pretending to erase a part of humanity that you'd rather not deal with.

Not even the illuminati at the NAACP and their mock funeral, a sterling example of theater of the absurd, can do this.

And now, six questions from Oneita the Language Provocateur:

1. Is not saying the word the same as not thinking it?
2. What is the value of giving that word the silent treatment if the principles of subject-verb agreement are a mystery to you?
3. Would you feel better if the person who shot you didn't call you that name?

4. Is not acknowledging your neighbor the same as not addressing him by that name?
5. What does it matter that the person who denied you a job didn't use the word when she told you you couldn't have a job, even though you were the most qualified?
6. What will happen when the NAACP leadership finds the stone rolled away from the sepulchre and they find not the body of the nigger?

## Oneita

It is absolutely none of my business, but I think you may be making a mistake in sending your son to a public school "of your choice". The world is a much stranger place than it was even when you went to school, and it might be better to send him to a charter school. This is not a racial thing. In light of the fact that he has expressed reservations about your choice for his future, he just may be too intelligent and emotionally mature to go to a public school. This may subject him to abuse from some or many of the other students, who will be jealous of him. They will make his life miserable. It is not true that putting an intelligent kid into an environment with a bunch of crude thugs will result in the less intelligent kids becoming better human beings. They will just try to drag him down to their level, or preferably, below it. That's just the way it is. I was there, so don't you dare try to tell me any different. It is misguided to try to make the world a better place and improve it by effectively sacrificing your child. It is also misguided to try to "toughen the kid up (like John Wayne)". He will either become less of a person, or very bitter. Your son will be exposed to the crude side of life soon enough; it is better to wait until he is mature enough to defend himself against it, physically and emotionally, and able to clearly recognize it for the depravity that it is.

I can only speak with certainly from my own experience, even though I have also seen the negative results in other people. I was born in 1950, and the only other reasonable educational options at that time were Catholic schools. I spent Kindergarten in an upper middle class city. I fit right in, since I was a self-motivated artsy type, even at that young age. The next year, my mom moved to a very lower class (southern white trash) city. I became a prisoner of war for the next twelve years. The neighbors literally hated my guts, and they passed this hate down to their children. Working together, these families made my life a living hell. There were even covenants in this city's deeds that prohibited the sale of homes to Italians. As a child, I had no idea that any of this was going on. I found out later in life (when one of the people who were adults during my youth let it slip out), how the adults were filled with jealousy, and how they handed down this raging anger to their children.

Last year, a mixed race couple (black man and white woman) came into the store where I was working. She mentioned that she was writing a book, and, since I'm also a writer, we started talking about things. I mentioned that I had lived down south for about ten years, and had noticed how most of the lower class whites there had incredibly huge chips on their shoulders, and were constantly angry, just like the southern white trash that I had grown up with. The man said that it was interesting that I had observed that constant level of anger in the people down there. We looked at each other and didn't say anything, but we both understood that he had gotten the worse treatment from these perpetually angry people.

As I said, it's none of my business where you choose to enroll your son in school. But, if you are trying to be noble, at his expense; that is to try to inject civility into an uncivil environment by placing him there, you are just sacrificing him, and possibly subjecting him to unnecessary permanent scarring. I never did finish high school. I got my GED later, and attended college. Putting me into that incredibly hostile environment did not raise the standards of my "peers". It did not make us all one big happy family. It was a total waste of my life.

In the "good old days", children, and women, did what they were told. They were seen, and not heard. The world has changed, and everybody who is old enough to realize where they are going deserves a chance to decide if they want to go there.

You do what you want. Just be ready to live with the possible consequences.

Thanks for your time. If you use any of this, please do not use my name.

**Where did you read that I was sending my son to a public school?**

"They can't even get to the real issues, the difficult stuff that should make us uncomfortable."

What makes me uncomfortable is my failing to understand why anyone would refer to Charles Barkley as a "role model". I think most people embrace their truths, however uncomfortable they are, not just Charles Barkley!

IMHO, the .."ingenious irony" is that a lot of what he says and does is precisely because he is as much of a racist as anyone. From calling folks whitey, to tossing them through windows. And then excusing himself (and being excused), either because of his fame/notoriety, or his playing the race card if you point out his boorish behavior.

I do agree that a lot of people would rather try to shout you down than offer sound logical reasoning to back up their position. It is usually those folks that have no position.

I appreciate your willingness to have meaningful conversations.

**Why do people become offended by truth? I just read "American White People Really Hate**

Being Called 'White People'" in Vox magazine. Why do white people become upset when you call them white? Why do fat chicks get mad when you say they're fat?

Dear Oneita,

    I enjoy your Sunday column very much.
I enjoy hearing about your son.

    This letter is in regard to your
column on June 21, Father's Day.

    Your friend talking about her culture
Irish Catholic this & Indian that but
she never says the word white.

    You mention the word Black. Why? You're
not black for 1 thing but brown. Can't you
refer to yourself as African American?

    I don't mean any disrespect and
please don't take me wrong. I have
trouble explaining myself.

                           Faithful Reader

**You explained yourself well, Faithful Reader.
Why do you have a problem with what I *do*
call myself and why do you feel compelled to
tell me what I *should* call myself? I don't mean
any disrespect and please don't take me wrong.
I think it is interesting that you did not pro-
vide a return address so you could receive a
response from me.**

Oneita, Please don't throw "black and African" in our faces. I am white Belgian,German decent. I do NOT think of myself as such, but I think of myself as an AMERICAN. I'm sure you were not born in Africa, therefore, you are American first. Thank you for letting me voice my opinion of your June 21, 2009 column in the Free Press.

**Let me throw this in your face, too: I am a writer, a mother, a daughter, a sister, a native Daytonian. I am short, right-handed, female, Spanish-speaking, English-speaking. I speak fluent ghetto. I am a glasses-wearer, a walker, bus rider, knitter. A nappy-headed, east-side Detroiter. ALL AT THE SAME TIME, nothing ordinal about it. Why do you have a problem with how I define myself? I think of who I am, not who I am NOT, and I am NOT Belgian, NOT of German descent. Acknowledging who I am is NOT my problem. It's yours. (And how are you sure you know what's on my birth certificate?)**

Oneita Jackson

How about a little trivia in regards to black history month? First, when are you and the NAACP going to have a funeral for all the bad words blacks call white people? And, why are you afraid to talk about all the white people murdered and raped by black thugs. Let's talk about all the bad black history—there's a lot of it out there. And why not mention that Martin Luther King was not a saint—far from it. In fact on the day he was shot, he was shacking up with a black woman, not his wife. This is documented.

And finally, if you want to find real racism: How about a white Detroiter running for mayor of Detroit. And why not try to get a column out without playing your race card.

*(The typewritten letter arrived with no return address; the reader attached a newspaper clipping with a photo of Georgia Powers and the caption below.)*

KING AFFAIR: Georgia Powers, Kentucky's first black state senator, says that she had a year-long relationship with the Rev. Martin Luther King Jr., and that she was with him the night before his April 4, 1968, assassination in Memphis. "It was not the greatest part of my life but it was something that happened," Powers, 71, writes in her autobiography I Shared the Dream. The Rev. Ralph Abernathy, King's associate, was criticized five years ago for suggesting in his memoirs that King had affairs. King's widow, Coretta Scott King, was unavailable for comment.

**A white man from Livonia is now the mayor of Detroit: We have overcome.**

I was wondering just how 'polite' the Detroiters who rioted in 1967 where while they burned down homes and businesses. I'm also wondering just how 'polite' the black folks who threw rocks at our car and glared at us from porches and street corners as we drove to my Grandparent's house in East Detroit a few years ago. I wonder how 'polite' the group of black workers at Metro Airport were to those of us walking down the terminal to get our luggage while 10 of these 'polite' workers walked in a straight line and as slow as they could while the polite black security guards looked on with smiles on their faces?

**Polite white people are all over the national news for calling 911 to dispatch the police on black people because they feel threatened by the mere *presence* of African Americans: an Oregon state representative campaigning in a neighborhood; a family of seven eating at a Subway in Coweta County, Georgia, and using its restroom; two men sitting at Starbucks in Philadelphia waiting for a meeting to start; five women golfers at the Grandview Golf course in York County, Pennsylvania; a boy mowing a lawn in Maple Heights, Ohio; a student at Yale asleep in the common area of**

her dorm; a Smith College student eating her lunch on campus; a woman at a Safeway in Mountain View, California, helping a homeless person; a woman swimming at a private pool in her Winston-Salem subdivision; a man wearing socks at a pool in Memphis; a pre-med student at a candy store in Santa Fe, New Mexico, whom the store clerk described as "black" and "arrogant."

Why didn't you call the police in East Detroit if you felt threatened? Why didn't you call the Detroit Metro Airport police if you felt uncomfortable? Why didn't you just say, "Excuse me, please," and go around the workers? I wrote "Politeness Just Won't Do in Response to Racism" after one of my white friends who works at a Ford plant asked me how to deal with one of his white coworkers who sent racist e-mails behind his other coworkers' backs right now, in the 21st Century. Why are you asking me about something that happened in the 20th Century? I wasn't even alive in 1967.

Oneita Jackson—

The biggest racists are those who go around calling other people racists, i.e., hypocritical blacks like you. You pick out one incident where a black was handcuffed and shot by a police officer in California—never mentioning all the thousands of whites who have been murdered, raped, carjacked, etc. by black thugs. It's blacks like you that keep the racist pot boiling.

**A BART officer shot and killed Oscar Grant in the back while he was handcuffed. I am the mother of a 24-year-old. Are you a parent? How would you feel if your 22-year-old son was shot in the back and killed by a transit police officer in Oakland—and a fellow parent, a newspaper columnist, wrote about it simply because she had compassion and empathy for you, love for humanity, and hope for justice?**

*Part Four*

People don't want the truth, they want to be angry.

"Tell them I'm black."

*Oneita, to her friend Muffy, before an event at a private Detroit club. She is the club's official cab driver, a friend of one of its members, and has been invited to attend special events at the all-white, all-male club during a competition all weekend long. She is the only black guest there. The Help, however, are all African-American men.*

"Did you tell them I was black?"

*Oneita, in a text to her friend Muffy, on the way to the event. Oneita was to go with Muffy & Co., but took too long getting dressed, so they left her. Oneita gives Muffy a detailed description of her ensemble: red wool blazer, black-and-white pattern dress with yellow trim; lattice tights; black kitten-heel pointy boots; short haircut; mismatched earrings; white flower bag with yellow dot. She wants to make sure the people at the club are expecting her. Muffy simply tells the men at the club her friend Oneita is coming. She later says she didn't think it was necessary to describe her friend as an African-American woman.*

"You didn't tell them I was black?"

*Oneita, to Muffy, after the event. When Oneita arrives at the club, she rings the doorbell as she had seen the baron from Montreal do. She had picked him up at the Windsor airport and dropped him off the previous day. A nice white man greets her and shows her in. This salutation is interrupted by a House Negro who suddenly appears to challenge her presence. "Excuse me, but can I help you?" the House Negro asks, looking Oneita up and down. Oneita feels defeated. "She didn't tell them I was black," she thinks. She extends her left arm, dramatically, brings her wrist under her nose, looks at her Swatch watch, glares at the House Negro, and explains her presence: "I am here for a match that began at 11:00. I realize it is 11:15, but"—the nice white man interrupts and welcomes her in.*

"Miss Oneita, would you like for me to call you-all a cab?"

*The House Negro who initially tried to block Oneita from entering the club, as Oneita leaves to take her fare back to her hotel. The woman, visiting from Philadelphia, is pissy drunk. During the evening, Oneita is recognized as the former Detroit Free Press O Street columnist and is received even more warmly by the club's perfect gentlemen. They argue over who is going to pay for her food. "Put it on my tab!" "No, put Oneita's food on my tab!" "Give her anything she wants—I'm paying for it!" The three House Negroes are in awe. Upon seeing this respect and admiration, House Negro No. 1 caters to her all night long. "Miss Oneita" this and "Miss Oneita" that. Oneita declines his offer of transportation. "No, thank you. I'm a cab driver."*

"How do you guys know each other?"

*Guest, to Oneita, at a Fourth of July party in downtown Detroit. Oneita is one of a few black people there and is greeted affectionately by several guests, including her friends who own Lafayette Laundry. "I wash," Oneita tells the white woman.*

"How do you know Joe?"

*Guest, to Oneita, at a Christmas party in the home of her good friend. "He's my friend," Oneita responds, smiling and nodding. She assumes all the guests know the hosts because the party is in their home. The middle-age white man, a music conductor, smiles and nods, too, though he says nothing. "Yes, he's my friend," Oneita repeats, still smiling and nodding. He seems to be waiting for more information—an explanation? "Oh, how do I know him?" Oneita says, and explains her presence in the home of a gay, white male couple. Oneita is the only black female, only heterosexual female, one of three black people there.*

"Is *that* how you know her?"

*Guest, to Oneita, after she recounts a story about visiting her friend's courtroom. They are at a 52nd birthday party for her friend, the judge, in her home in West Village, Detroit, and argue about where her 50th birthday party was held. The guests are lawyers, doctors, business owners, and other Very Important People in the city of Detroit. It is the first time the well-dressed, middle-age African-American man has visited the home, but not Oneita's. She tells him there was a private 50th birthday party in her home; he attended the party at her cousin's club, TV Lounge. All night, the man has been trying to figure out how Oneita, a Detroit cab driver, knows the 36th District judge. "What do you do?" he asks, then, "Are you family?" He never asks, "How do you know Cylenthia?"*

"How do you know Berg?"

*Oneita's neighbor, a white woman, inquiring about Oneita's friendship with another neighbor, an Egyptian man. He lives across the street from the woman; they are both homeowners in West Village, Detroit. Oneita is a renter who has lived in the neighborhood 17 years and knows Berg, who works bare-chested in his yard as long as the weather permits. Oneita does not understand the question. "He's my neighbor," she responds.*

"I don't think they have the type of food you're looking for."

*Hotel employee, to Oneita, at the Marriott in downtown Detroit. She is waiting to get a hug from the Indian hugging saint, Amma, and has been told there is delicious Indian food on another floor, so she leaves to find it. "Is this the floor where the food is?" she asks a millennial African-American man. When he responds, Oneita says, "Well, why don't you tell me what kind of food I am looking for?"*

"Why do you need credentials for the auto show?"

*Detroit Free Press business editor, a white man, to Oneita, a news copy editor who has been writing a popular blog for a few months. Oneita wants to write about the Charity Preview, an annual black tie event she usually attends as a guest. She has never attended as a member of the media and has never written about it. She feels she does not have to justify her request to the editor and never responds. He becomes sick and Oneita is given his tickets to the event. Her fashion blog about the event is one of the most-read articles on the newspaper website; her photo of Aretha Franklin runs on the front page of the Detroit Free Press. The newspaper had sent its entire staff of photographers and photo editors to the event—it even hired freelancers—but only Oneita photographs the Queen of Soul. An award-winning photographer criticizes the photo. "What photo of Aretha Franklin did you take?" Oneita asks him.*

"How did you hear about this?"

*Free Press pop music columnist, a white man, upon seeing Oneita in an editorial meeting with radio and music industry professionals, including Dionne Warwick and Mary Wilson of the Supremes. "How did you hear about this?" Oneita thinks. "I wrote a column about the radio industry Sunday," she says.*

"We have more in common than you might think."

*Mother of Oneita's friend, who is visiting Detroit from Los Angeles. He wants them to meet because his mother is an aspiring writer. Oneita is happy to talk about her love of English and of crafting sentences. She first asks the little old white lady from the suburbs, "How do you know what I think?" The woman bumbles through an explanation about what she perceives Oneita might perceive. Oneita exchanges contact information with her friend's mother and recommends books about writing, but Oneita never hears from either of them again.*

"This table is for family."

*Church member, upon seeing Oneita and her son seated at a table that is reserved for the pastor after morning worship. Oneita grew up with the pastor in Dayton, Ohio, and his family is visiting Detroit from there. She is talking with one of her pastor's four brothers when the church member interrupts. "I am family," Oneita says.*

"What time is the bus picking y'all up?"

*Deacon, mistaking church member Oneita for one of the homeless guests the church hosted overnight. When Oneita arrives late for her volunteer shift in the middle of the night, she is told there is nothing for her to do until morning, so she goes to sleep on a cot where the guests are. In the morning, she is assigned to toiletry duty; the deacon monitors her as she presents toiletry bags to the guests. She has no name tag, one, the deacon doesn't know her, two, and she is wearing her street urchin clothes, three, so she understands the mistake. "I don't know, I drove," she tells him. "This one here say she drove," he yells to other church members; they are scrambling to feed the guests before they depart. Oneita is amused. She knows what the deacon will ask next and he does: "What kind of car you drive?"*

"We're closed for a private event."

*White millennial young woman at Bookies Bar & Grille in downtown Detroit, upon seeing Oneita, who is there for the private event.*

"You've really stepped up your wardrobe."

*Oneita's hairdresser's boyfriend's sister, who has begun to ride the Metro bus Oneita takes on her way to work in Georgetown, Washington. She is used to seeing Oneita sitting under a hair dryer at the salon wearing cut-off shorts and a T-shirt. "I am going to work," Oneita responds.*

"If I were a white man from Philadelphia wearing a suit and was a curator, would you be trying to help me right now?"

*Oneita, to a security guard, at the Detroit Institute of Arts. "Yes," he says. Oneita is the fixer for a team of journalists from Spanish Public Television and has dropped them off to interview the DIA director, Salvador Salort-Pons. When she enters the museum, the guard offers no assistance. He does not know where the journalists are, he says, and does not try to find them. Oneita calls her friend Kenneth Morris, the museum's director of evaluation and research. He is on the way and will take her to the crew from Madrid, Spain. While Oneita waits, she interrogates the young black man. She respects his honesty.*

"Let me take you to a seat up front so you can hear the speaker better."

*Member of the Detroit Rotary Club, to Oneita, at a weekly luncheon at the Detroit Athletic Club. Oneita has not visited the DAC since the time she was disrespected while trying to valet her taxicab. "I'll be doing the speaking today," she says to the woman, one of a few black members of the club. Oneita has been invited by her friend, an older white woman, to address the group. Oneita's picture is on its website.*

"Good for you."

*Cab customer, to Oneita, as she drives him to the airport. They are having a conversation about education when she tells him her son attended an all-boys Jesuit high school in Detroit. "Why is that good for me?" she asks the young white man. "I did not go to an all-boys Jesuit school. I simply sent him to one."*

"Good for you."

*Cab customer, to Oneita, on the way to Detroit Metro airport. During the three years Oneita has been a cab driver, she has had conversations with many kinds of people from many countries—six continents—about many subjects. On this day, she and her fare are talking about education. Oneita tells him her son attended an all-boys Jesuit high school in Detroit. "Why is that good for me?" she asks the middle-age white man. "I did not attend an all-boys Jesuit school."*

"Good for you."

*Cab customer, to Oneita, as she drives him to the airport. They are having a conversation about education when she tells the older white man her son attended an all-boys Jesuit high school in Detroit. "Why is that good for me?" she asks. "I did not attend an all-boys Jesuit school."*

"Good for *him*."

*Cab customer, to Oneita, on the way to the airport. They are having a conversation about education. She tells him that her son attended an all-boys Jesuit high school in Detroit. She also tells him how white men have responded: "Good for you." They all said she was a good mother who valued her son's education and that she should be proud. Oneita and her fare, a black man around her age, laugh at the white men's responses.*

"You need to get better at reading white privilege, because I'm a white male and that's what that was!"

*Former Detroit Free Press publisher Dave Hunke, one of Oneita's regular fares, during a standoff on a one-way street on the side of the YMCA in downtown Detroit. Oneita is driving Hunke, as he was called in the newsroom, to the airport. The white man driving is telling Oneita to move with what she learns later is called the "white privilege wave." Oneita has driven down the street for years. She looks left, then right, then looks for signs to see if the street has become a two-way street. It hasn't.*

"That's called the 'white privilege wave.'"

*Pulitzer Prize winner Jim Schaefer, explaining the hand motion to a fascinated Oneita, who cannot believe there is a name for it. She calls her former Detroit Free Press colleague, the least pretentious white man she knows. "That's the thing you do when you're standing at the gas pump and you look at the guy like, 'Turn this thing on.'"*

"That's because you look like Tyrone and sound like Hosni Mubarak."

*Oneita, to her friend Maged Zaher, a Seattle poet. He tells Oneita he just greeted some young African-American guys outside his downtown Detroit hotel and that one of them said, "What the fuck are you?" under his breath. Oneita's friend wears locks and looks like a light-skinned, African-American surfer dude. He is a surfer dude, but he is not from the United States. He is from Egypt and has a hard accent. That means he doesn't say, "Hi, guys." He says, "Hoi, goize."*

"Are you waiting for the bus?"

*Black man who presents as a drunkard, seeing Oneita in an elegant black dress, at the Rosa Parks Bus Terminal in downtown Detroit. She has just gotten off work at Grey Ghost, a slick New American restaurant in Brush Park, Detroit. It is late on a Sunday night. Detroit's buses are notoriously late, especially at night and on Sundays. "Are you waiting for the bus?" he asks Oneita again— there are several other people at the bus stop. "I'm at the bus stop!" she yells.*

One time I was at the bus stop and a man asked me if I was waiting for the bus.

I was waiting for the pelicans.

One time I was at a ninth-grade orientation for my son and a man asked me if I was there for the ninth-grade orientation.

I was there for the pelicans.

One time I was at a paper store called the Paper Store and a Paper Store employee asked me if I was there to buy paper.

I was there to buy pelicans.

"Do you own this place?"

*Customer, to Oneita, at Selden Standard, a slick New American restaurant in Cass Corridor, Detroit. He approaches her with a smile and points to the ceiling, making circles. Then he points at her. She gasps. "Sir, I am going to hug you right now and then I will tell you why." Oneita hugs the handsome, middle-age white man, and explains. "I have never been mistaken as the owner of some white-privilege shit in my whole life!" The man thinks he has offended Oneita and he apologizes. No apologies needed, Oneita says. She has been mistaken for a lot of other things in her life, but not this. They talk for the duration of the evening. She tells him about the Preview Edition of Nappy-Headed Negro Syndrome and asks why he thought she owned the place. He says he has been watching her move about the restaurant with confidence. She is greeting people—several of her friends are there, even some of her cab fares from earlier in the day. "You look like you have your shit together."*

*Part Five*

The problem of the 21st Century
is willful ignorance.

## American Badass

Kid Rock opened Little Caesars Arena, home of the Detroit Pistons and Detroit Red Wings, with a concert that provoked much tumult and shouting in Motown, a city whose population is 83% African American: The born-near-Detroit native supports President Donald J. Trump, has been known to fly a Confederate flag at his concerts, and he is white.

*My* problem with the September 12, 2017, show was that I had about 15 minutes to get to LCA before it would end. I am not a native Detroiter, so I have no fond memories of going to see the Pistons play at the Superdome or watching a hockey game at the Joe Louis Arena. That is why I was walking urgently, because I did not want to miss history, and that is precisely why the security guard said he stopped me.

I had just gotten off work at Grey Ghost Detroit, where I was a hostess, and was wearing a fancy black dress, my Stars and Stripes, high-top Converse, and my red-white-and-blue 25th Anniversary Swatch. I heard the guard running behind me—he was panting by the time he caught up—but I ignored him.

"Excuse me, ma'am! Miss, miss!" I heard him saying something in his walkie-talkie.

"WHAT do you want?" I asked the guard. He looked like the Human Beat Box.

"Um, where you going?"

"I AM GOING TO THE CONCERT."

"Oh. Well, I stopped you because you were walking so fast."

"You stopped me because I was walking too fast? I AM TRYING TO GET INTO THE SHOW."

To the surprise of my ears, the four-person Welcome Committee at the turnstiles told me the show was over.

"The concert is not over. I can hear the music, and I need to get in."

I showed them my ticket and demanded they let me in. One woman told me they put the scanners away.

"You need to go get whoever is in charge and tell them to let me in."

A friendly supervisor arrived.

She scanned my ticket, and I went in.

I had to see for myself, up close and personal, how Trump got elected.

## What Happened in Vegas

The concierge was a beautiful twentysomething, dark-hair Filipino woman with a Farrah Fawcett flip haircut, a well-tailored suit, elegant chrome nails and a flawlessly made-up face that cracked nary a smile.

She was stunning, so stunning, perfectly petite and poised, that she could not hand me a newspaper.

I was in Las Vegas for a book-signing when I sauntered into the concierge space at the SLS hotel, saw a stack of Wall Street Journals and got excited.

"May I have one of those, please?" I asked. The newspapers were on a table behind her to the left. If she had yawned, she could have grabbed the whole stack.

"You're free to take one," she said.

I looked at her, then at the Wall Street Journals, then back at her.

"I'm free to take one?"

"Yes, you're free to take one."

I used to be a concierge at the Discovery Channel Building and the Bethesda Place Apartments in Bethesda, Maryland, and it was one of my favorite jobs. It was a joy to serve the people there, to exceed their expectations, and to help them as much as I could. I researched information, planned parties, did errands, and planned events as a proud member of Classic Concierge.

My request required no effort, but there was no newspaper presented to me.

Filipino Farrah sighed her way through my next question, about downtown bookstores, grudgingly writing the name of the nearest one. She challenged me when I asked her about the location of Writer's Block, which is owned by a friend of a friend.

"You *said* the nearest bookstore," she chided, "and that is *not* the nearest bookstore."

Oh, my.

I thanked her for the information and decided to give her one more opportunity to be a stellar representative of the profession I used to belong to.

"Will you hand me a Wall Street Journal, please?"

"You're free to take one."

I took one, folded it in half, and stuck it right beneath her uppity nose.

"I used to be a concierge," I said. "And if one of my guests had asked me for a newspaper, I would have handed them one."

The next day I returned to the concierge desk dressed the same way I was the day before, wearing sweatpants, a T-shirt, and sneakers. The concierge was a handsome, thirtysomething white South African gentleman named Travis.

We laughed about our respective African heritages, and when I asked him for a Wall Street Journal, he handed me one.

## What Registers

What is your expectation if you are standing at a cash register?

I'm from Dayton, Ohio, home of NCR and Standard Register, so I know cash register etiquette: Stand anywhere in the vicinity of one, and a friendly sales associate will appear to help you.

That didn't happen to me at the Denver airport.

I got off my flight and headed straight to the Hudson News stand, where I waited longer than I should have, to be acknowledged. I had been watching the thirtysomething cashier watch me watch her as she moved boxes and straightened out one stack, then another, of magazines.

When she thought I had been standing at the cash register too long, I reckon, she made her way over to me.

"Do you need something?" the Ethiopian-looking woman asked.

This transported me to Baltimore, where I had another encounter with another Ethiopian-looking woman at another cash register—at another Hudson News stand.

I had placed my magazine on the counter when the older woman tapped it and said, "It's eight dollars."

I smiled the cheesy smile I've come to perfect when I am amused, and gave her a jussive nod, which meant, "Ring it up."

"What is in this magazine that you're paying eight dollars for it?" she demanded.

"This," I said, pointing to "The War on Stupid People." It was on the cover of the Atlantic magazine and I directed her to read it: She worked at a newsstand.

The woman at the newsstand in Denver saw me standing at the cash register and asked me if I needed something.

"Do you need me to stand somewhere else?"

My question was earnest; hers, inscrutable.

## The Spook Who Stood by the Door

Everyone who worked at Grey Ghost Detroit wore black, cap-sleeve, silkscreen T-shirts with a white Grey Ghost logo; jeans, sneakers, and custom-made leather aprons: the servers, the server assistants, dishwashers, chefs, bartenders, bar backs, the chef-owners.

I didn't.

I wore fancy black dresses. There was no formal dress code for hostesses, but I implemented my own, established when I worked at another Detroit restaurant: I wore black. Black is my favorite color, so I was always in uniform.

Being a restaurant hostess was exciting. I enjoyed solving problems and making people feel good in my designer clothes. (I usually walk around Detroit in my street urchin clothes: dirty T-shirt, baggy sweatpants or cut-off shorts, run-down sneakers.)

Working at Grey Ghost was interesting.

The Brush Park restaurant has a cool name, a cool story, and a telegenic staff. It is new-Detroit slick

and hip and loud. People have to wait weeks, some-
times months, for a reservation because everyone
wants to eat at a cool restaurant in Detroit at the
same time. The headlines contribute to its intrigue.
Urban explorers and Detroit Tigers and Detroit
Lions fans sit next to prominent people from all
over the world who sit next to local and national
celebrities: Detroit media darlings Rhonda Walker
and Diana Lewis and her daughter, Glenda Lewis.
Sports icons Dave Bing, Joe Dumars, Tony Hawk.
From Hollywood: Eric Benet and Samantha Ware.
And Dan Gilbert of Quicken Loans and the Cleve-
land Cavaliers.

One of my friends came in wearing shorts and a
tether.

The funniest people were the people from Detroit
Mayor Mike Duggan's office who used to *try* to use
their status as public servants of the City of Detroit
to secure a table, tsk-tsk, and the people who like to
be impressed with themselves, like the group from
Anna Purna pictures that made the movie "Detroit."
They had to let everyone know they were in the
restaurant. When Dan Gilbert dined, no one even
knew he was there and *he* has an advance team and
a bodyguard.

My job as the baddest little hostess in Detroit was especially fascinating because I was the only African-American woman who worked there. Ninety percent of the staff and its customers were white. I learned a lot about people by observing how they responded to my uniform. I was always happily overdressed, relishing in my sartorial brilliance—I'm pleased with myself, too—because putting together my outfits was another outlet for my creativity.

Three Japanese women walked in the door one day.

"You're wearing a kimono!" one said. "She's wearing a kimono!" the woman said to the other two. My kimono kissed the floor as I moved. I was wearing double-panel palazzo pants, too, and Japanese-style sneakers with a horse-hoof toe. I caught the mighty-real Sylvester spirit and spun around like Diana Ross in "Mahogany."

"Yes, I *am* wearing a kimono!"

\*\*\*

When I wore Burberry, the compliments from white women were amusing. They were always the same, whether I had on my black, button-front, tartan-collar coat dress or my tan, red-black-and-cream vertical-stripe, vintage wool blazer. (I rarely deviated from my standard black, but I always in uniform.)

"It looks like Burberry," they'd say, mispronouncing the name as Shaquithianetta would.

BURR-BEAR-REE.

One shift, I had a record night: compliments from four different broads!

"I like your blazer. It looks like Burberry."

I thanked the first three, but lost my grace with the fourth.

"I like your blazer," the millennial woman said. "It looks like Burberry."

"*Does* it?"

I smiled my cheesy smile and nodded.

"Yes," she said.

"*Really?*"

"Yeah, you should tell people it's Burberry."

"I *should?*"

"Yes!"

"It *is.*"

\*\*\*

My uniform threw people off, like the impeccably dressed older white women from Grosse Pointe.

They were sharp and I told them so. Their table wasn't ready, so their husbands stood to the side while we chatted. The women admired my style, too. I told them about my dress and my shoes. They thought my chain coin belt was fancy; it was a gift from my friend Kristalé, I told them, who bought it in Paris.

"Oh?" one said, raising her eyebrows. She turned to her friend.

"You mean Paris, *Texas?*" she said.

They snickered.

Paris, *Texas?*

I swallowed, I enunciated.

"France."

I was talking about Paris—Paris, *France.*

I had never heard of Paris, Texas, so I looked it up when I got off work.

The city of about 25,000 has a 65-foot Eiffel Tower. One of the Oak Ridge Boys went to school in Paris; I grew up listening to the Oak Ridge Boys. John Osteen was born there; I like his son Joel Osteen. Paris, Texas, has a history of racial hostility and is known for lynching black people. I *had* heard of Paris, Texas. It is the place where two white men ran over Brandon McClelland and dragged him to his death in 2009, leaving his body so dismembered that it couldn't be embalmed.

One of the husbands stepped over, pointed his thumb at me.

"Do you know who this woman is?"

I have a keyring that cracks me up; it reads: "Do you

know who the fuck I am?" (I also have Eiffel tower keyrings, gifts from my editor, Alex, and my best friend, Jamilah, whose mother is from Paris—Paris, France.)

The man began to recite the Complete Edition of my résumé.

I was more shocked than his wife and her friend.

\*\*\*

The man on the patio wanted another drink.

"I'll let your server know," I said.

I had gone out there to check on our guests. I loved mingling with them, learning about them.

"You're not my server?"

"No, sir, but I will go get your server and let her know."

"Wait, *you're* not my server?" the man on the patio said.

"No, sir, but I will make sure she knows."

"I thought *you* were my server?"

"No, sir, I'm not."

The man on the patio had been straddling the park bench. He shook his head, swung his left leg over the bench, and finally sat his ass down.

The beautiful Stephanie León arrived.

"*Here* is your server," I said, with a Vanna White smile.

Stephanie León is a fair-skinned Mexican woman and she is about four inches shorter than I. She has a Serena Williams beauty mark between her upper lip and left nostril.

\*\*\*

The woman ordered the highest steak on the menu and complained about its price to me as she and her husband were on their way out the door.

"I see why more of us don't come in here," she said. She had an Anita Baker haircut and she and her husband looked like they were going to a cabaret.

I did not tell that woman to order the fifty-five dollar steak. I always told people to order the cheeseburger, which is like a slick Big Mac. It is the best burger in Detroit and it costs thirteen dollars.

\*\*\*

My friend Jeanette Pierce tagged me in a June 14, 2017, Facebook post her friend wrote about a fracas at the restaurant with some baseball fans.

Jeanette is Caucasian American; her friend is South Asian American. Her friend posted:

"Next time I see you, remind me to tell you about that one time/thirty minutes ago when I got in a verbal altercation with with a bunch of drunk Tigers fans, because one of them muttered to me that he deemed the bartender "a toothless nigg\*r for not serving him a burger AFTER the kitchen had been closed. Good seeing you tonight, Pierce. Sorry about the commotion."

Jeanette: "Holy shit! Were we still there when that happened? We didn't hear/notice anything outside otherwise I probably would have made a larger commotion having your and the Bartender's back! Also if **Oneita Jackson** had still been there ... that would have been something too!"

Friend: "Maybe you had gone, because those yahoos were complaining that the patio was closed too."

So I posted: "That toothless nigger is a University of Detroit Jesuit graduate. Allow me to introduce myself: I'm the nigger at the front door. I'm sorry you had that experience. I was gone by then, but yes, **Jeanette** is right: I would have checked them with grace."

My coworker-the-bartender was my son's UDJ high school classmate, and like him, knows home training. He is a perspicacious bartender, able to sustain conversations with international visitors. He is an intellectual and is doe-eyed handsome. He was in a life-threatening accident, though, that caused injuries that required, among other things, multiple dental surgeries.

He wasn't wearing his flipper fronts that night with his uniform.

## Know Home Training

The woman at the salad bar told me her name was Wendy.

She and her family were sitting at a table a few feet from me—two cute, school-age boys, her husband, her parents, the grands.

We were a table of about 20 celebrating my friend Enré's daughter Sierra's Sweet 16th birthday in Royal Oak, a close suburb of Detroit. I had never been to a Mongolian Grill, but White Wendy and her inferior powers of observation made the occasion memorable.

I approached White Wendy about 30 minutes after our salad bar encounter; I waited because I did not want to lose my grace.

Every time I put my chopsticks in my mouth, I thought about how I would communicate my disapproval of her rebuke of me. I thought about what she might be teaching those blond-hair boys—or what she wasn't. Those innocent boys would grow up to be white men. What kind of men would they grow up to be? I thought about my 24-year-old son, who has grown up to be a remarkable young man, and I thought about the lessons I imparted to him about making observations and about making assumptions. They lead people to conclude things that might not be true.

I walked up behind White Wendy and handed her my card.

"Hi," I said, with a reassuring smile. "I'm the girl from the salad bar."

I nodded at each of the five family members.

"Yes," she said, turning to me.

"I wrote a book about something like we experienced at the salad bar. I also wrote a book about bad customer service."

"OK," she said, looking at the card.

"E-mail me and I will send you PDFs of both books."

"OK," she said, and thanked me.

I knew White Wendy wouldn't e-mail me, and she didn't, but let me tell you what happened at the salad bar, when she was on liquid condiment patrol.

White Wendy saw me dip a white miniature plastic spoon into one of the salad dressings.

"DON'T!"

I swallowed.

White Wendy's hand demanded I stop. She looked at me with unbelievable disgust. I looked at her with piercing frigidity.

"Don't WHAT?" I said, punctuating my disdain by enunciating the alveolar "t."

"Don't put that in there after you put it in your mouth!"

I drew my spoons like John Wayne in a shoot-'em-up movie.

"I have *two*, lady," I said.

## Hotter than July

Riding the DDOT bus has been the single most frustrating, challenging, and incomprehensible experience of my 17-year Motor City existence. In real cities, public transportation works well, but not in Detroit, and it hasn't changed significantly through four mayors: Kwame Kilpatrick, Kenneth Cockrel Jr., Dave Bing, or Mike Duggan.

The buses are often late and raggedy, smelly and filthy.

The drivers are often unprofessional, discourteous, and unhelpful.

The passengers—mostly lower-income black people—are often disruptive, like the woman who was sitting next to me in the back of the bus one Sunday when I was headed to church. It was an unusually great experience: The bus was on time, the driver was one I knew (friendly, professional), the bus was clean, and the air conditioning was working on an oppressive summer day.

I was reading my New York Times when a guy brushed past me to take the left window seat in the back of the bus. The disruptive woman was sitting in the right window seat; I was in my favorite seat, the middle. I love sitting in the back of the bus because I like to see everything that's going on. (I sit in the back of the church, too.) There were two men sitting in the right and left side seats near us.

I stopped reading my newspaper and waited for an "excuse me."

I didn't hear one.

I looked the young man up and down for three seconds—he was oblivious I was looking at him—then went back to reading my paper. He was quiet and focused the entire ride.

Bless his heart, I thought, he seemed to have a lot on his mind.

The woman to my right, however, was not quiet, at all, and was focused on me. I felt her watching me watch him.

I kept reading.

"She must ain't hear him say, 'Excuse me,'" she said.

She got the attention of the two men in the side seats.

"I said that she must ain't hear him say, 'Excuse me,'" she said, attempting, I reckon, to elicit a response from me.

The older men looked at her.

I remained focused.

"This one," she said, pointing too closely to me.

I was reading "Oakland in Their Bones, and in Their Films," about "Blindspotting," which stars Daveed Diggs and Rafael Casal, and Boots Riley's film "Sorry to Bother You," which stars Lakeith Stansfield. Both movies are about identity, judgment, and assumptions. I took out a pen and made notes about the article and about her.

She looked me up and down.

My ignoring her seemed to incite her to be bolder. She had one more time to encroach, I thought, before I would lay these big-ass hands on her.

"She all saditty. Look at her."

*I got your saditty right here.*

"Who?" one man asked.

"This one."

She called me saditty, yes, she did, and she started signifying something terrible, launching into an eight-minute diatribe about people who think they are better than others.

her rich uncle was rich and he had a lot of money but lost it and he had to come back to the hood because he had forgotten who he was and she couldn't stand him and that is what is wrong with people who think they are better than you and they don't need to ever forget where they came from and who does she think she is look at her reading her newspaper got her nose all stuck up in the air thanking she better than everybody and she ain't shit and that's what happen to people she on this bus like the rest of us and she up here thanking she all that look at her she don't even know who she is ...

*I don't know who I am?*

I didn't know who I was?

That there was hilarious.

I am a black girl from the west side of Dayton, Ohio, who spent her summers in gritty New York City, and lived in the hood in Washington, D.C., and until recently, lived in West Village, on the east side of Detroit.

*Don't let this newspaper stuff fool you.*

I.

Went.

Off.

"I'm homeless!"

I jumped in her face.

"I'M HOMELESS, OK?"

The bus hushed.

The men sat up.

"I'M BACK HERE READING MY PAPER, MIND-ING MY BUSINESS, AND YOU RUNNING

YOUR MOUTH AND YOU DON'T EVEN KNOW
NOTHING ABOUT ME!"

"Well, why you ain't just say that? Why you ain't just
say you was homeless?"

"I AIN'T GOTTA EXPLAIN MYSELF TO **YOU**!"

I could roll my neck like all ghetto girls.

"I RIDE THIS BUS EVERY DAMN DAY. I GOT
MY BUS PASS, I'M MINDING MY BUSINESS
AND I'M TRYING TO GET TO CHURCH, AND
YOU NEED TO SHUT UP TALKING ABOUT
PEOPLE AND YOU DON'T KNOW NOTHING
ABOUT THEM. I SPOKE TO YOU WHEN I GOT
ON THE BUS. I SAID, 'HOW ARE YOU?' AND
I ASKED YOU WHAT KIND OF CANDY YOU
WERE EATING."

I thought she had some Mike & Ike's, which I liked.

The bus got quieter, so did she, but she would not
relent, telling me not to tell her to shut up.

"YOU NEED TO LEAVE ME ALONE, OK? I'M
TRYING TO GET TO CHURCH."

The driver stopped the bus.

What's that fuss coming from the back of the bus?

"Nothing is going on back here!" I yelled. "We straight."

"I wasn't talking about you," the driver said.

"Oh, I'm the one who was causing all the commotion, driver. I apologize. I'm just trying to get to church."

The bus started rolling.

Back to my paper.

"Well, I didn't know she was homeless," the woman said, then started talking about homeless people.

I wasn't finished with her.

"YEAH, AND YOU SEE THESE GLASSES?" I pointed at the lenses. "DO YOU SEE THESE BIFOCALS ON MY FACE?"

I was in her face again.

"MY NOSE IS IN THE AIR BECAUSE I CAIN'T SEE, OK? YEAH, MY NOSE IS IN THE AIR. I JUST STARTED WEARING GLASSES AND I. CAIN'T. SEE."

I went back to my newspaper and ignored her the rest of the trip.

she doesn't have to be homeless there is all kinds of help out here for homeless people i didn't know she was homeless there is a place right down there on the boulevard that can help people and it's a lot of us out here who need help and there ain't nothing to be ashamed about i try to help as many people as i can and i go to church too and she ain't gotta be out here by herself somebody can help her . . .

When I got up to exit the bus, the people smiled and told me to have a good day at church.

## Nappy-Headed Negro Syndrome

The man buying buttons at the bookstore thought I should be flattered by his thinking I was the cashier, but I wasn't.

I have aspired to many things, but cashier is not one of them—not that there's anything wrong with being a cashier.

When I was a cab driver, people would ask me what I did for a living. "Oh, there's nothing wrong with that," they would say. There was nothing wrong with their being a teacher or a lawyer or a senior vice president or a biologist or a minister or a pharmaceutical sales rep or a business owner, either, just like there isn't anything wrong with being a cashier.

But I wasn't a cashier.

I have been a cashier, but I wasn't one that day.

I was helping Leni Sinclair. The photographer, almost 80 years old, is a Detroit legend. My claim to fame right now is that I carried Leni Sinclair's milk crate. I met her in the parking lot as she carried her framed prints and notecards of music giants: John

Coltrane, Marvin Gaye, Prince, the Rolling Stones, the Beatles, Aretha Franklin.

It was hotter than July in August. I had on cut-off pants and a muscle T-shirt.

We were at a suburban bookstore that was celebrating its 36th anniversary with an event on National Book Lovers Day. The owner and his wife were featured in Newsweek. There were authors and musicians and other artists coming and going all day; they would be open until midnight. I was not part of the event because the owner told me he wanted to host a book-signing to coincide with the release of this book, the Complete Edition of *Nappy-Headed Negro Syndrome*, and that he should have invited me. I was just happy to be there—the bookstore was the only bookstore in the Detroit area carrying my book—and I told him so. My friend and I had stopped by the Book Beat so I could sign copies of *Letters from Mrs. Grundy*.

I'd been sitting outside the bookstore at the table vacated by the authors Shelley Johannes and Christopher Paul Curtis, when the owner walked over and said, "Leni Sinclair is coming."

I gasped.

"Really? This day cannot get any better," I said.

When I met Curtis, I was overcome: He and I have a connection to Dave Eggers, we do, but I was standing next to the man whose books were on my son's bookshelf. The author of *The Watsons Go to Birmingham* and *Bud, Not Buddy* was sitting right in front of me. We took pictures—"I can't wait to tell my son I met you!" I gave the Newbery winner and Johannes first-edition, out-of-print copies of my book about bad customer service, which I grabbed when I left home. They gave me copies of *their* books: *The Mighty Miss Malone* and *Beatrice Zinker, Upside Down Thinker*.

\*\*\*

I am hanging with Leni Sinclair.

A woman who knows her from way back when approaches. "It's Leni Sinclair," I say. The woman knows it's Leni Sinclair. While they talk, I offer to help her place her notecards, lining them up across the table.

A Leni Sinclair groupie with a goofy smile walks up.

He flips through the photos, then sorts through the buttons.

"How much are the buttons?" he asks me.

I look at Leni.

"How much are the buttons, Leni? The man is asking how much the buttons are."

She tells him they cost one dollar.

I am pleased with my arrangement, so I sit at the end of the table.

The man offers me three dollars.

I moveth not. There are three white women waiting for the man: wife, mother, sister/sister-in-law, I reckon. He nods, insisting I take the money.

"Give it to *her*."

I direct him to Leni, as a "Price Is Right" Showcase model would.

He steps toward me. I glare at him. He steps toward Leni. She takes the money. He and that goofy smile walk toward me.

"I thought you were the cashier."

I swallow my insolence, stand up, and enunciate, one two, three:

"I am *not* the cashier.

"I am an *author*.

"You can buy autographed copies of my *books* inside."

The man buying the buttons and the three women behind him stare at me.

I do not look like a "Price Is Right" model.

\*\*\*

"I can take the next person in line," the cashier says.

I am smiling and waiting to be acknowledged, but the cashier is talking to the older white woman behind me. I allow my face to turn slightly left, so I can glance over my shoulder. The woman behind me knows she bet' not move and she doesn't. I'm next. "Go ahead," she says. I inhale, forcing the cashier, a twentysomething black woman, to be present during this inconvenient moment of truth: I am not with the older black woman in front of me.

She is embarrassed.

My smile is forgiving.

\*\*\*

Leni Sinclair was surprised I knew who she was.

She asked me who *I* was.

"Oh, I'm no one," I said. I'm just happy to be here."

"Everybody does something," she said, flipping through her prints, which were matted and on sale for twenty-five dollars: Iggy Pop, the MC5, Bob Seger. (The woman who knew Leni from way back had pointed to the poster of Seger in the window. "Look, Leni," she said. Leni stopped setting up, looked at it, and said, "Mine is better.")

Hashtag: Truth.

"What do you do?" she asked me. Leni Sinclair had an accent. I'd never heard her talk; I knew her only through her work.

I told her I was a writer and that I stopped by to sign my books. I told her that I was having so much fun I decided to stay. I was meeting Leni Sinclair and the day could not get any better I told her.

It did.

She asked me about *Letters from Mrs. Grundy* and told me she would buy it.

"It's twelve dollars and fifty-five cents," I told her, and directed her inside to pay for it. She said OK and told me to choose three of her note cards, which were five dollars apiece.

I looked for photos of black artists—Leni photographed legends—and chose one of Aretha Franklin. *I wonder how she is doing?*

\*\*\*

The bookstore owner approaches the table, sees what he thinks is attempted barter, chastises me and her or me or her: "What's going on? I sell books. You can't barter. I sell these books."

He takes the book off the table.

I do not understand and I do not like his tone. I assure him that there is no bartering going on.

"Leni told me she would buy my book," I tell him. I thought she offered me the postcards because I helped her set up her table.

"She doesn't have any money," he says.

"I didn't tell you that," I say.

"No, *she* doesn't," the bookstore owner says. "Leni doesn't have any money."

"OK," I say. "I can send her a PDF. I give everyone PDFs of my books."

"Do you hear that, Leni? She wants to send you a PDF of her book for your postcards," he says.

"I don't need a postcard!" I yell, throwing my hands in the air. I have enough postcards, notecards, specialty paper, ink pens and postage stamps to open my own paper store.

The bookstore owner takes the book inside.

Leni says nothing.

I gather my things, but not quickly enough.

The bookstore owner returns.

"Oneita, I want to make sure we get off on the right foot," he says. The words coming out of his mouth and the expression on his face do not match.

"Yes," I say—he cuts me off.

"Let me finish."

His tone demands I stand more erectly, stare him square in the eyes, and listen while he plumb insults me.

"I want to make sure we get off on the right foot, OK? I told you we were going to do a signing for you when the new *Nappy-Headed Negro Syndrome* comes out. I didn't invite you to this because I wanted to focus on the new book.... but trying to hustle Leni Sinclair—that was just low. NO ONE HUSTLES LENI SINCLAIR, OK? That was low."

I swallow.

"May I speak now? Are you finished?"

"Yes, go ahead."

"I did not try to hustle Leni Sinclair."

"Yes, you did."

"No, I did not."

"Yes, you did. You tried to give her a PDF for her postcards."

Before I know it, my E.T. Phone Home finger is a quarter of an inch from his face, pointing straight up in the air, telling him to stop in the name of truth, daring him to say another motherfucking word.

"I don't know who you *think* I am," I said, "but I am not a liar, I am not a thief."

"OK."

I choke up, but dare a tear to fall.

"I was a Detroit Free Press copy editor for 11 years and a columnist."

"Oh-kaaay."

"I did not try to hustle Leni Sinclair. She told me she was going to buy my book."

"OK—she *did?*"

"Yes. Leni Sinclair told me she was going to buy my book. I told her it was twelve dollars and fifty-five cents and that she could pay for it inside—the same as I have been telling everyone else. I have been sending them inside to buy the book."

The shipment of eight books arrived the day before; there were six when I got there, two when I left.

He comes closer.

"Yeah, but she doesn't have any money," he whispers. "Leni doesn't have any money," he says, and begins to tell me Leni Sinclair's business, which is none of mine.

The E.T. Phone Home finger.

"I don't know that, and it is none of my business."

"OK."

He nods and walks away.

"Let's get outta here," I say to my friend, whom I find inside the store.

I have just enough dignity and composure to make it to the car, where I will sob the entire way home, traumatized by this experience of my burnt sienna existence.

The bookstore owner's wife stops me on the way out to ask about the release of this book. She thanks me for stopping by and I hug her. "Should we call you or you will call us when the book comes out?"

Her husband is sitting outside.

I extend my hand.

"Thanks, Oneita."

You're welcome.

*Contact photographer Leni Sinclair at lenisinclair@hotmail.com.*

This book was completed after the deaths of Aretha Franklin and John McCain. Watching their services left me with indelible impressions of why it is important to pay attention and to mind your manners. Amen.

**Oneita Jackson** is a Detroit satirist who has an English degree from Howard University.

She was a copy editor for 11 years at the Detroit Free Press. During that time, she served as public editor, wrote music reviews, edited on the Features, Nation/World, and Web desks, and received awards for her headline-writing. She emerged as a leader on the News Copy Desk, conducting workshops, speaking to students, and presenting at seminars. She was a member of the Accuracy and Credibility Committee and the Editorial Endorsement Board for the 2008 City of Detroit mayoral and City Council elections. She also wrote O Street for three years. It received the newspaper's 2008 Columnist of the Year award.

She stopped writing the column in May 2010 and returned to the News Copy Desk, where she stayed until August 2012.

Her next adventure was driving a yellow cab. She was featured in the local and international media ("First Block," HOUR Detroit, "Under the Radar: Michigan," Al Jazeera English) for her unique approach to the job. Mercedes-Benz International honored her on its She's Mercedes platform.

She was also a professional fixer during that time, working with international journalists, including teams from Paris, France (Le Petit Journal); Madrid, Spain (TVE-Television España); Copenhagen, Denmark (Jyllands-Posten), and Montreal, Quebec (Radio Canada). She also worked with an executive team from Martha Stewart.

She has worked in fine dining and fast food restaurants in Detroit as a manager, hostess, barback, cashier, and dishwasher. She consults in the restaurant and hospitality industry now, focusing on customer service and etiquette through the lenses of her books.

The Dayton, Ohio, native spent her summers in New York City and has lived in Washington, D.C., and Albany, N.Y. Her family is from Birmingham, Alabama. She still has a passion for newspapers and is often asked to guest-lecture to journalism classes when she's not crafting sentences to leave a literary legacy for her son, Jay.